THE SFORZA
HOURS

THE SFORZA HOURS

Mark Evans

THE BRITISH LIBRARY

In memory of
JOAN EVANS
(1925–1978)

Front Cover: Enlarged detail of fig. 49.

Back Cover: Enlarged detail of Sforza Hours
(British Library Add. MS 34294, f. 334r).

Half-title: (fig. 1) Birago: *May,* detached
miniature from the Calendar of the Sforza Hours
(British Library Add. MS 62997r). Actual size.

Frontispiece: Enlargement of fig. 50.

First published 1992 by
The British Library, Great Russell Street,
London WC1B 3DG

Cataloguing in Publication Data is available from
The British Library

ISBN 0 7123 0268 9

Photography by Annie Gilbert

Designed by James Shurmer

Typeset in Linotron 300 Bembo
by Bexhill Phototypesetters, Bexhill-on-Sea

Printed in England by Balding + Mansell,
Wisbech

CONTENTS

THE HISTORY OF THE
SFORZA HOURS

In 1895 the connoisseur J. C. Robinson, now best known for laying the foundations of the collection of Italian Renaissance sculpture at the Victoria and Albert Museum, recalled his discovery of the Sforza Hours.

In 1870 the land route to Spain was virtually closed by the [Franco-Prussian] war, and in 1871, during the German occupation and the second (Communist) siege of Paris, it was only by very roundabout roads that the country betwixt Calais and the Pyrenees could be traversed. However, in October 1871, I made my way to Spain...

The time was especially propitious for the acquisition of works of art... for the ubiquitous French dealers were nearly all shut up in the beleaguered city, and their Spanish colleagues were only too eager to welcome any clients who might present themselves in such a time of depression...

A few days after my arrival in Madrid, whilst staying at Don José's hotel, that worthy individual... said that some months previously a priest one day had brought him a wonderful illuminated manuscript – something overwhelming, *un preciosidad sin ugual,* ... He was the agent,

(*Left*)
2 Birago: *October*, detached miniature from the Calendar of the Sforza Hours (Coll. B. Breslauer, New York).

(*Right*)
3 Birago: *St John*, Gospel Lessons (fol. 1r).

probably the family chaplain, of a great personage, who, in the usual custom of Spain, desired to remain incognito. He was commissioned to sell the book for a fixed price, no less than twenty thousand pesetas, or eight hundred pounds sterling... finally, Don José made up his mind to give the required thousands. These, in the shape of notes of the bank of Madrid, he one day put into the pocket of his 'capa', that fine old picturesque brown 'paño pardo' cloak, without which no true Spaniard ever goes into the street in Madrid. Thus attired, he duly sallied out to go to the residence of the priest and conclude the bargain; unluckily the good father was not at home, and Don José had to return... not thinking of the notes in the pocket of his cloak, he hung that garment up in the common-room of his own hotel, intending to go again to the priest's house in an hour or two's time, but when the time came and he arrived there for the second time, – when the book was in his hands, – his own in fact, as he thought, the cup was cruelly dashed from his lips at the very moment of anticipated enjoyment, for, on feeling in his pocket for the 20,000 pesetas, lo! they were nowhere to be found; some thief had abstracted them during the brief time that his cloak had been hanging up in his public room... This story excited me not a little, and I forthwith engaged Don José to get me sight of the ill-omened treasure; this he undertook to do, and the very same evening he brought the priest to my room, when with much ceremony the little corpulent velvet-covered volume was put into my hands. The very first page opened, disclosing two glorious illuminations, blazing with colours and gold, struck me dumb with admiration, but when every page of the book, and there were more than two hundred of them, was revealed equally enriched, the only thought was that it should not again for an instant leave my hands; and literally it did not, for luckily I had provided the funds in anticipation and so the bargain was instantly concluded. No entreaty could induce the vendor to give any information as to the previous ownership or history of the book, although I left no means of persuasion untried. Don José received a handsome gratuity by way of commission from me, and I hope he also received something from the owner of the book, though as to that I am very doubtful.

On his return home, Robinson offered the hours to the British Museum, but the Treasury refused to meet his price and the manuscript was acquired by the wealthy Argyll landowner and enthusiastic collector of Old Master drawings and manuscript cuttings, John Malcolm of Poltalloch. In 1893, shortly before his death, Malcolm presented it to the British Museum, which acknowledged his generosity the following year with the publication of G. F. Warner's monograph on the hours. In this exemplary study, Warner divined its Milanese origins from the miniature on fol. 14v celebrating St Barnabas as the first to celebrate Mass in Milan and the text of the prayer to St Ambrose, the patron saint of the city, on fol. 198r. He identified Bona of Savoy (d. 1503), the wife of Galeazzo Maria Sforza, Duke of Milan 1466–76, and mother of Gian Galeazzo, Duke of Milan 1476–94, as its original owner from the device of the phoenix with the motto *Sola facta, solum Deum sequor* on fol. 93r and the inscriptions *Diva Bona, Bona Duc*[issa] and *B.M.* on various folios.

In his study, Warner drew attention to a fifteenth-century letter from the Milanese illuminator and priest Giovan Pietro Birago to a head of state or other notable, which had been published in 1885. Neither the date nor the addressee was given in the document, which claimed that:

The incomplete book of hours, which was recently presented to your Excellency, was stolen from me by Fra Johanne Jacopo, a friar in the convent of San Marco at Milan. The aforementioned is in the prison of the Rocha de Porta Nova. The aforementioned book of hours is that which

Duchess Bona had made. Payment of 1220 lire [the lire was a money of account of a variable value relative to the gold ducat] is due to me for the above. The part which your excellency has is worth more than 500 ducats. The other part is with the illustrious Duchess... I beg your Excellency not to permit the said Fra Johane Jacopo to be released until he has paid for the said book of hours and provided satisfaction for the damage and the interest sustained by the said crime....

Even permitting some exaggeration in this 'insurance valuation' of the stolen part at 500 ducats – five times Leonardo da Vinci's own estimate in 1504–06 of the value of his *Virgin of the Rocks* – Birago's huge estimate indicates that the decoration of the manuscript was spectacular. Despite its fragmentary condition, associations with the Duchess Bona Sforza and exceptionally rich decoration, Warner refrained from the conclusion that the Sforza Hours was identical with the mutilated book mentioned in the letter. It was only in 1956 that the discovery of his signature on the illuminated frontispiece of a volume of Giovanni Simonetta's *Sforziada*, printed at Milan in 1490, emancipated Birago from the name of convenience 'Master of the Sforza Hours'.

We do not know if Birago ever received compensation for the theft of part of the Sforza Hours, but the stolen folios were never returned. When discovered, the book lacked a calendar, although two full-page miniatures from this have recently come to

4 Birago: *St Luke*, Gospel Lessons
(fol. 4r).

n ullo tpe.

n ullo .

tt z sermonem confir
mante: sequentibus
signis. Deo gracias.

Omine iesu
christe fili dei
uiui pone pas
sionem cruce z mo:
tem tuam inter iudi
cium tuu et anima
mea nunc z in hora
mortis mee. z mihi
largiri digneris gra
tiam z misericordia
uiuis z defunctis re

(*Above*) 7 Horenbout: *St Mark*, Gospel Lessons (fol. 10v [enlarged]).

(*Opposite, top left*) 5 Birago: *St Matthew*, Gospel Lessons (fol. 7r).

(*Opposite, top right*) 6 Horenbout: *St Mark*, Gospel Lessons (fol. 10v).

(*Opposite, bottom left*) 8 Horenbout: *Christ nailed to the Cross*, Hours of the Cross (fol. 12v).

(*Opposite, bottom right*) 9 Birago: Decorated border with vignette of St Barnabas, Hours of the Cross (fol. 14v).

light. Nearly a third of its 348 folios are replacements which competently, if rather shakily, imitate the original neat rounded gothic script. It seems likely that Bona had abandoned the project by 1494, the year in which her son Gian Galeazzo died and his uncle Ludovico il Moro assumed the title of Duke of Milan, brushing aside the claim of her young grandson Francesco Sforza. Excluded from power by her brother-in-law, Bona returned to her native Savoy in 1495 as the guest of her nephew, Duke Phillibert II. On her death at Fossano in 1503 the unfinished manuscript was apparently inherited by Phillibert, who died the following year. The book of hours then became the property of his widow, Margaret of Austria, who moved to the Netherlands in 1506 as Regent for her young nephew, the future Emperor Charles V.

The manuscript languished until 1517, in which year the domestic accounts of the house of Savoy record Margaret's payment of the scribe Etienne de Lale

for his pain and trouble in having written several vellum leaves for those hours, made in the Italian style and with Italian pictures, which came from the late madame Bonne of Milan, which hours had lost the said leaves in various places, and is now put back in order.

The accounts for January 1521 record further payments to the miniaturist Gerard Horenbout;

First, for having made sixteen beautiful miniatures well illuminated to match the rich hours on parchment for my said lady... 60 livres... for having made for the said hours seven hundred golden letters... four livres 4 sols [1 livre = 20 sols]... to pay the said Master Girard for writing some leaves of those hours... 40 sols... for having made two text illustrations for my said lady in those hours... 56 sols.

The Sforza House was thus completed. Its subsequent history is unknown until 1871. One of Horenbout's text illustrations is a portrait of Charles V, dated 1520, the year of his coronation as Emperor. Accordingly, the book may have been completed as a gift for Margaret's nephew. Such a provenance would account for its removal to Charles's favourite kingdom of Castile, where it was discovered by Robinson 350 years later.

THE INITIATION OF THE SFORZA HOURS: BONA SFORZA AND RENAISSANCE MILAN

The first decorated books of hours date from the thirteenth century, when the 'little office' or hours of the Virgin Mary was emancipated from a subordinate role as an appendix of the Psalter to constitute a prayer book for the laity. Its full artistic potential was demonstrated at the turn of the fourteenth and fifteenth centuries in a series of large volumes richly decorated by the court miniaturists of the French Duke Jean de Berry (1340–1416), which remain the most celebrated of all books of hours.

Bona Sforza was originally from Savoy and spent her last years there. In 1485–89, shortly before Birago began her book of hours, Bona's nephew Charles I of Savoy (d.1489) commissioned Jean Colombe to complete the *Très Riches Heures* (Chantilly, Musée Condé, Ms 65), left unfinished on the death of his ancestor Jean de Berry. The exceptionally rich decorative programme of the Sforza Hours may have been intended to equal that of the *Très Riches Heures* itself.

Both Jean de Berry and his brother Charles V, King of France (1338–1380), assembled magnificent libraries. Their principal rival as a bibliophile was Giangaleazzo Visconti, Count and later first Duke of Milan (1351–1402), who founded the great library at Pavia. This was augmented by his successors and comprised over a thousand volumes by 1499 when it was seized by the invading Louis XII and a large part of it united with the French royal library.

During the Quattrocento, the success and diffusion of the new humanist culture in Italy encouraged the growth of more comprehensive libraries, embracing classical philosophers, poets, orators, grammarians, historians and natural scientists, as well as liturgical books and the works of Christian theologians, philosophers, poets and other writers. The inventory of new additions to the Milanese ducal library during the decade 1459–69 lists 123 new titles, most of which were classical texts or recent works by humanist authors. In France and the Netherlands during the fifteenth century wealthy patrons had access to a much narrower range of reading-matter, in which prayer books were of paramount importance. As a result, the decorated book of hours never dominated the market in illuminated manuscripts in Italy in the same way as it did in Northern Europe.

Moreover, the most elaborate books of hours required such an extravagant expenditure

10 Birago: *Descent of the Holy Spirit*,
Hours of the Holy Spirit (fol. 28r).

13

(*Above, left*)
11 Birago: Decorated border with vignette of musical angel, Hours of the Holy Spirit (fol. 38r).

(*Above, right*)
12 Horenbout: *Annunciation*, Hours of the Virgin (fol. 41r).

(*Right*)
13 Horenbout: Decorated border with vignette of rabbits, Hours of the Virgin (fol. 48r).

(*Above, left*)
14 Birago: Decorated border with vignette of female saint and peacocks, Hours of the Virgin (fol. 54r).

(*Above, right*)
15 Horenbout: *Visitation*, Hours of the Virgin (fol. 61r).

(*Right*)
16 Birago: Decorated border with text as placard flanked by putti, Hours of the Virgin (fol. 73r).

of time and effort that they remained quintessentially a form of court art. In this context, it is telling to consider the group of prayer books commissioned towards the end of his life by Lorenzo de' Medici (1449–1492), effective head of state of still republican Florence. Although of superlative quality, both in decoration and calligraphy, each has no more than five openings with full-page miniatures facing decorated folios. In the Duchy of Milan, a 'benchmark' for the genre was provided by the composite psalter and hours with over 60 full-page miniatures and nearly a hundred ornately decorated pages, begun for Giangaleazzo Visconti around 1388 and finished for his son Filippo Maria (1392–1447) some 40 years later (Florence, Biblioteca Nazionale Ms Banco Rari 397 and Landau-Finaly 22). Bona Sforza may also have wished to surpass this spectacular volume.

The miniaturist who completed the Visconti Hours, Belbello da Pavia, enjoyed a considerable reputation in the north Italian courts during the first half of the Quattrocento, subsequently decorating a *Bible historiale* (Biblioteca Vaticana, Barb. Lat. 613) for Niccolò d'Este, Marquis of Ferrara (1383–1441). The copy of Plutarch's *Lives* decorated by him in the British Library (Add. MS 22318) indicates that, like the painter Pisanello, whom he worked beside at Mantua during the 1450s, Belbello established a partial *rapprochement* with the increasingly fashonable classicism emanating from Padua. In 1456 the invitation from Marquis Ludovico Gonzaga (1412–1478) to the young Paduan Andrea Mantegna to be court painter at Mantua was a watershed in the North Italian Renaissance. Court taste changed rapidly. Six years later Ludovico's wife Barbara of Brandenburg refused Belbello's request to complete, without payment, a missal he had begun but which had been transferred on Mantegna's advice to his own follower Girolamo da Cremona.

Mantegna's style had already been introduced to Lombardy by Vincenzo Foppa, resident at Pavia from 1458. A Brescian probably trained in Padua, he was employed by Galeazzo Maria Sforza and was well established at court by the time of the Duke's marriage to Bona in 1468. A letter of 1480 from the Marquis of Mantua, Federico I Gonzaga (1441–84), to the Duchess indicates Bona's own taste both for the Mantegnesque and for small-scale painting:

Most illustrious Excellency, I have received the portrait painting that your Excellency sent me and have done my utmost to make Mantegna make a small reproduction in elegant form. He says this would almost be the work of a miniature-painter, and because he is not accustomed to painting small figures he would much rather do a Madonna, or something the length of a *braccia* or a *braccia* and a half [*c*.63.8 cm. or 95.7 cm.], if it were pleasing to Your Most Illustrious Highness. My Lady, if I might know what your Ladyship wants me to do, I shall endeavour to satisfy your wish, but usually these painters have a touch of the fantastic and it is advisable to take what they offer one...

The altogether more autocratic tone of communications from Galeazzo Maria Sforza and Ludovico il Moro to Vincenzo Foppa suggests that such whims would not have been tolerated from painters at the Milanese court. Giovan Pietro Birago was a more amenable courtier, as is indicated by the overtly propagandist nature of his *Sforziada* frontispieces for Ludovico il Moro. Birago's personality, as well as his skill as a miniaturist in the

North Italian antiquarian style pioneered by Mantegna, would have recommended him to Bona for such an ambitious project as the Sforza Hours.

GIOVAN PIETRO BIRAGO

The date and place of his birth are unknown, but his name suggests he was from Birago, a town near Milan, or that he was from a Milanese family of this name. On several occasions he signed himself 'Presbiter', indicating that he was a priest. Birago's earliest known works are several signed miniatures in choir books from Brescia Cathedral, dated 1471/74 (Brescia, Pinacoteca Tosio Martinengo, nn. 22, 23 and 25). Miniatures attributed to him appear in a breviary of the Venetian Barozzo family, printed in 1481 (Vienna, Österreichische Nationalbibliothek, Inc. 4.H 63) and it has been proposed that he was working in Venice during the 1480s. By about 1490 he was the leading miniaturist at the Sforza court and most of his chief works were executed in Milan towards the end of the Quattrocento. Francesco Binasco, an illuminator, engraver and jeweller and a favourite of Ludovico il Moro's son Francesco Maria Sforza (1495–1535), was probably trained in Birago's workshop.

The Sforza Hours is his masterpiece. Also for Bona Sforza, he participated in the decoration of a *Legenda de Sancto Iosaphat* (Milan, Biblioteca Baidense, MS ACX I, 37). For Bona's rival Ludovico il Moro, Birago executed ornate illuminated frontispieces in a series of deluxe copies, printed on vellum in 1490, of Giovanni Simonetta's *Sforziada*, a life of Francesco Sforza, the founder of the Sforza dynasty in Milan. Ludovico's own copy is in the British Library (Grenville 7251) and that presented to his nephew and predecessor as duke, Gian Galeazzo, is in the Bibliothèque Nationale in Paris (Imprimés, Réserve, Vélins 724). A copy in the Biblioteka Narodowa, Warsaw (Inc. F. 1347) with a signed frontispiece was a gift to the general Galeazzo da Sanseverino, who married Ludovico's illegitimate daughter Bianca in 1496. Nine fragments from the frontispiece of a fourth *Sforziada* in the Uffizi (Inv. 1890, nn. 843 and 4423–4430) include another signature by the artist. Also in Florence (Biblioteca Riccardiana, ed. v. 428) is a copy of the 1486 Latin edition of the *Sforziada* with a frontispiece and a full page miniature of Francesco Sforza on horseback by Birago. This bears the Imperial arms and was probably presented to Maximilian I on his marriage to Maria Bianca Sforza in 1494. She was probably the owner of the small volume of Italian sonnets and songs with two exquisite miniatures by Birago in Wolfenbüttel (Herzog August Bibliothek, Cod. Guelf. 277.4 Extr.).

Birago contributed to the decoration of two books for Massimiliano Sforza, the younger son of Ludovico; a copy of Aelius Donatus, *Ars Minor* and the *Liber Iesus*, both in the Biblioteca Trivulziana in Milan (codice no. 2167 and 2163). His workshop was responsible for the mutilated Hours of Francesco Maria Sforza, of 1491–94, and a decorated marriage grant of 1494 from Ludovico il Moro to his wife Beatrice d'Este, both in the British Library (Add. MS 63493 and Add. MS 21413). He was also an engraver, to whom have been attributed six engravings of religious subjects, two of *putti* and a series of twelve upright ornamental panels.

(*Above, left*)
17 Horenbout: *Nativity, at Night*, Hours of the Virgin
(fol. 82v).

(*Above, right*)
18 Birago: Decorated border with vignette of *putto* playing
with rabbits, Hours of the Virgin (fol. 84v).

(*Right*)
19 Horenbout: *Annunciation to the Shepherds*, Hours of the
Virgin (fol. 91r).

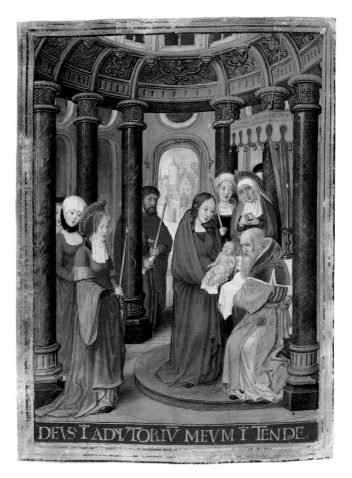

(*Above, left*)
20 Birago: *Adoration of the Magi*, detached miniature from the Hours of the Virgin of the Sforza Hours (British Library Add. MS 45722r).

(*Above, right*)
21 Horenbout: *Adoration of the Magi*, Hours of the Virgin (fol. 97r).

(*Right*)
22 Horenbout: *Presentation in the Temple*, Hours of the Virgin (fol. 104v).

23 Horenbout: *Flight into Egypt*, Hours of the Virgin (fol. 111r).

24 Horenbout: *Coronation of the Virgin by the Trinity*, Hours of the Virgin (fol. 124r).

25 Horenbout: *Virgin and Child in Glory*, accessory prayer 'Salve Regina' (fol. 133v).

26 Horenbout: *Entry into Jerusalem*, Passion according to St Luke (fol. 136v).

27 Birago: *Payment of Judas*, Passion according to St Luke (fol. 137r).

28 Birago: *Last Supper*, Passion according to St Luke (fol. 138v).

(*Above, left*)
29 Birago: *Agony in the Garden*, Passion according to St Luke
(fol. 145v).

(*Above, right*)
30 Birago: *Arrest of Christ*, Passion according to St Luke
(fol. 147v).

(*Right*)
31 Birago: *Christ before Annanias*, Passion according to St Luke
(fol. 149v).

The recipients of Birago's last known works reflect the increasingly precarious position of the Sforza state after the first French invasion of Italy in 1494. These are a small book of hours presented by Ludovico il Moro to Charles VIII of France (Venice, Coll. Cini) and a volume of biographies of French kings by Alberto Cattaneo of Piacenza, destined for Charles VIII, but probably presented after his death to Louis XII (Paris, Bibliothèque de l'Arsenal, ms. 1096). Birago survived the invasion of Milan in 1499 and the capture of his former employer Ludovico in 1500, just as he had done the fall of Bona Sforza in 1494. In 1506 Louis XII, as Duke of Milan, granted him a copyright. He is last heard of in an autograph letter, dated 6 April 1513.

THE COMPLETION OF THE SFORZA HOURS: MARGARET OF AUSTRIA AND THE RENAISSANCE IN THE NETHERLANDS

Despite leading indirectly to the creation of the sumptuous Bedford Hours (London, British Library Add. MS 18850), the English occupation of Paris in 1420 had a generally disastrous effect on the school of illumination which had flourished there at the turn of the fourteenth and fifteenth centuries. While the first Valois Dukes of Burgundy, Philip the Bold (1342–1404) and John the Fearless (1371–1417) had been essentially French royal princes, their successors Philip the Good (1396–1467) and Charles the Bold (1433–1477) became increasingly independent rulers, living mainly in their rich Netherlandish territories. This political change and its attendant concentration of patronage was a major factor in the effloresence of the Netherlandish school of painting during the fifteenth century.

Philip the Good greatly expanded the Burgundian Library and commissioned a large book of hours, profusely illustrated in grisaille (The Hague, Koninklijke Bibliotheek, ms. 76.f.2). His son Charles the Bold was also a connoisseur, who owned several luxurious 'black' books of hours, with text written in gold and silver on leaves stained black or purple. Charles gave one of these (Vienna, Österreichische Nationalbibliothek, Cod. 1856) to Galeazzo Maria Sforza (1444–1476), the husband of Bona Sforza, probably during their brief alliance of 1475–76. The daughter and heir of Duke Charles, Mary of Burgundy (1457–1482) shared his taste for fine manuscripts, as is evident from her own hours (Vienna, Österreichische Nationalbibliothek, Cod. 1857), from which is derived the name of a leading anonymous painter of the Ghent-Bruges School, the 'Master of Mary of Burgundy'. Her husband Maximilian, Archduke of Austria and later Holy Roman Emperor (1459–1519), inherited the Burgundian Library together with Mary's Netherlandish territories following her death in 1482.

Maximilian also owned a book of hours (Vienna, Österreichische Nationalbibliothek, Cod. 1907) after which a major member of the Ghent-Bruges School is known, the 'Master of the Older Prayerbook of Emperor Maximilian'. His second marriage, to Ludovico il Moro's daughter Maria Bianca Sforza in 1494, led to his employment of the Milanese painter and miniaturist Giovanni Ambrogio Preda. It also probably resulted in the arrival at the Habsburg court of at least two books decorated by Giovan Pietro

Birago, the volume of sonnets and songs in Wolfenbüttel and the *Sforziada* in the Biblioteca Ricardiana. The latter, one of a small, deluxe edition printed on vellum and hand decorated, may be a source of inspiration behind the celebrated *Prayer Book of Maximilian I*. This was printed in 1513 in a vellum edition of only five known copies, of which Maximilian's was decorated with drawings in coloured ink by Albrecht Dürer and Lucas Cranach (Munich, Bayerische Staatsbibliothek, 2 L.impr.membr.64).

The daughter of Maximilian and Mary of Burgundy, Margaret of Austria (1480–1530), inherited the Sforza Hours and probably the *Très Riches Heures* on the death of her husband Phillibert, Duke of Savoy, in 1504. Given her family background it is perhaps unsurprising that she became one of the greatest patrons of the Northern Renaissance after moving to the Netherlands as Regent in 1506. Margaret's collection included old masters, such as the *Arnolfini Wedding* by Jan van Eyck, the favourite artist of her great grandfather Philip the Good. She commissioned from Jean Perréal and Conrad Meit the splendid marble and alabaster tombs for herself and her husband at Brou. Her court painters included, in addition to Gerard Horenbout, the itinerant Venetian Jacopo de'Barbari and the Netherlanders Bernart van Orley, Jan Mostaert, Jan Gossaert and Jan Vermeyen. By 1521, the year in which Dürer marvelled over her many 'precious things,

32 Birago: *Christ before Caiaphas*,
Passion according to St Luke
(fol. 151v).

33 Birago: *Ecce Homo*, Passion
according to St Luke (fol. 153v).

34 Birago: *Crucifixion*, Passion
according to St Luke (fol. 161r).

35 Birago: *Pieta*, Passion according to
St Luke (fol. 165r).

36 Birago: *Mass of St Gregory*, Seven
Prayers of St Gregory (fol. 167r).

and precious library', Malines was one of the principal centres for the diffusion of the new Italianate style. At her court, the 30-year old Milanese miniatures in the Sforza Hours seemed eminently fashionable and the book a desirable subject for imitation and completion.

GERARD HORENBOUT

Horenbout became a master painter at Ghent in 1487. In 1498 and 1502 he engaged apprentice illuminators. He executed a cycle of tapestry cartoons in 1508–09 and in 1510–11 was paid by the municipal authorities for preparing a 'description', probably a large painting, of part of the city and its surroundings. In 1515 Margaret of Austria appointed him court painter. He remained resident at Ghent, but attended the Regent at her court in Malines whenever required. Between 1516 and 1522 he is documented as having executed various works for her, including a book of hours in 1517 and a portrait of Christian II of Denmark in 1522. However, his only surviving documented works are the 16 miniatures and two text illustrations added to the Sforza Hours. These include the dates 1519 and 1520 and were paid for in 1521.

Horenbout has been plausibly but not conclusively identified with the Master of James IV of Scotland, a leading miniaturist of the Ghent-Bruges School named after a book of hours made for this king in 1503–13 (Vienna, Österreichische Nationalbibliothek, Cod. 1897). The Master was responsible for several distinguished commissions, including the magnificent calendar cycle inspired by the *Très Riches Heures* in the Grimani Breviary of *c.*1515 (Venice, Biblioteca Marciana, Ms. Lat. XI 67 (7531) and large parts of the Spinola Hours of *c.*1515 (Malibu, J. Paul Getty Museum, Ms. Ludwig IX 18), the Rothschild Prayer Book of *c.*1510 (Vienna, Österreichische Nationalbibliothek, Cod. Ser. n. 2844), and the Breviary of Queen Isabella of Castile of *c.*1497 (London, British Library Add. MS 18851). Unlike the works attributed to the Master of James IV of Scotland, Horenbout's additions to the Sforza Hours are distinctly Italianate, drawing upon contemporary masters of the Antwerp School as well as Birago's earlier miniatures. This variance probably reveals a deliberate attempt to complement the older part of the book. A small panel painting of the *Ecce Homo* in the Národynyí Galerie in Prague has also been attributed to Horenbout.

In May 1521 Albrecht Dürer, on a visit to Antwerp, was greatly impressed by the skill of Horenbout's daughter Susanna as an illuminator. Not long after, Horenbout and his family emigrated to Britain. Susanna married John Parker, Yeoman of Henry VIII's Wardrobe of Robes and Keeper of the Palace of Westminster, and subsequently attended on both Anne of Cleves and Catherine Parr. From 1525 until his death in 1544 her brother Lucas was a leading court painter and a pioneer of that most characteristic Tudor art form, the portrait miniature. Between 1528 and 1531 their father Gerard Horenbout is also documented as a painter in the service of Henry VIII. A record of payment of duty on his estate in Ghent indicates that he died in 1540/41.

THE CALENDAR

Like most books of hours, the Sforza Hours was intended to open with a liturgical calendar to indicate the dates of feasts of the Church and of saints. When it was discovered, this element of the hours was missing, implying that it had belonged to the stolen part of the manuscript valued at 500 ducats which Birago mentioned in his letter of complaint. An article published in 1960 noted that two calendar miniatures from the Sforza Hours were in the collection of the book dealer Tammaro de Marinis. These are probably identical with two full-page miniatures discovered recently. One, depicting *May*, was acquired by the British Library in 1984 (Add. MS. 62997, *see* fig. 1) and the other, of the month *October*, is in the collection of B. H. Breslauer (*see* fig. 2).

Although in poor condition, these miniatures provide crucial information on the missing calendar of the Sforza Hours. Their versos bear the last third of the calendar text for the previous month; 20–30 April and 20–30 September. Each month would have consisted of a full-page miniature on the verso of a leaf, followed by three text pages: a total of 25 folios, taking into account the first recto and the last verso, both of which would have been blank. The April fragment commemorates Bishop Marcellinus of Embrun (20), St George (24), the Evangelist Mark (25) and St Peter Martyr (29) while the September fragment commemorates the Evangelist Matthew (21), St Maurice and Companions (22), Saints Cosmas and Damian (27), the Archangel Michael (29) and St Jerome (30). The names of St Matthew and the Archangel Michael are written in red, indicating their special importance to Bona Sforza.

The *May* miniature depicts an elegantly dressed young gentleman seated by a rose bush and a stream before a dwarf offering a dish, three young women proffering chaplets of roses, and five young men, some playing musical instruments and singing. In the background landscape, a peasant cuts grass with a scythe while another carries two baskets suspended from a pole over his shoulder. Haymaking is a common subject for *June* miniatures in French calendars, but could have been seasonal for May in Italy, on account of the warmer climate south of the Alps.

In the *October* miniature, the foreground is occupied by a young noble couple out hawking on horseback, accompanied by two grooms on foot and a pair of hunting dogs. The lady has cast her falcon, which is swooping on a small bird, while her companion holds his hawk at the ready. In the background, beyond a winding stream, a group of peasants attend to the vintage. Two carry containers for the grape harvest on their backs and four man a mechanical wine press, while a colleague samples the new wine flowing from the vat. Vintage scenes are common in calendar miniatures of *October* but scenes of riders hawking were more usual for April. Of particular interest are the massive steeds of the two riders. With flowing manes and pricked up ears, champing at the bit as their leg muscles swell with a purposeful stride, these horses recall the mount of Francesco Sforza in Birago's miniature from the frontispiece of the Emperor Maximilian's *Sforziada*. Their common probable source is the celebrated lost monumental clay model made by Leonardo da Vinci for the Sforza Monument commissioned by Ludovico il Moro but never completed.

(*Above, left*)
37 Birago: *Assumption of the Virgin*, 'Obsecro te' (fol. 170r).

(*Right*)
38 Birago: *Assumption of the Virgin*, 'Obsecro te' (fol. 170r [enlarged]).

(*Above, right*)
39 Horenbout: *Virgin and Child*, 'O intemerata' (fol. 177v).

(*Left*)
40 Birago: *St Michael*, Suffrages (fol. 186v).

OBSECRO

Cycles of full-page calendar miniatures are very rare in fifteenth-century prayer books. Another unusual characteristic of the rediscovered scenes of *May* and *October* is their combination of aristocratic pastimes with peasant labours – an idea first employed in several of the full-page calendar miniatures from the *Très Riches Heures*. This analogy corroborates the proposal that the *Très Riches Heures* was a specific influence on the Sforza Hours.

THE GOSPEL LESSONS

Lessons selected from the four Gospels are a common element in books of hours. Their customary sequence is not that followed in the New Testament, but: John, Luke, Matthew and Mark. In the Sforza Hours each lesson is preceded by a portrait of the relevant Evangelist at work on his Gospel. Although half the folios of the Gospel Lessons are replacements, three of Birago's miniatures remain. These are of uneven quality, suggesting a high level of studio participation.

St John appears on fol. 1r (fig. 3), seated on the rocky island of Patmos before a scroll inscribed with the opening line of his Gospel: 'In the beginning was the Word'. In the foreground are a pheasant and a pair of ermines, creatures symbolic of purity which appear throughout the Sforza Hours. On fol. 4r St Luke is accompanied by his emblem of the Ox, studiously writing down the words of the Virgin Mary (fig. 4). This scene probably derives from the legend, frequently depicted by artists, that St Luke had painted a portrait of the Virgin. The male saint reading at the right is probably his companion, St Paul, whose life St Luke recorded in The Acts of the Apostles. *St Matthew* on fol. 7r is the most ambitious composition of the group (fig. 5). The saint is seated at a desk inscribed with his initials *S.M,* reading a book held by his symbol of an angel, within a cross-vaulted hall. The interior is buttressed by massive coffered barrel vaults which recall the classicising churches built by Donato Bramante in Milan during the 1480s and 1490s.

St Matthew's setting clearly influenced that of Horenbout's miniature of St Mark on fol. 10v (figs 6 and 7). Accompanied by his emblematic Lion, this Evangelist wears the soft cap and fur-trimmed gown of a Ghent bourgeois beneath his green robe and is seated before a fantastic arcade of blue columns encrusted with gilt decoration in the latest Italianate fashion. The transverse barrel vault at top left bears a cryptic inscription: NRVAS:FNOARVIMI:1519. The length of the two words suggests that this may be a cipher of the artist's name, followed by the date of the miniature's execution: LVCAS:HORENBOVT:1519.

THE HOURS OF THE CROSS

The Hours of the Cross is a customary component of books of hours. Illustrated versions of these prayers traditionally have a single miniature. Horenbout's picture added at its start on fol. 12v depicts *Christ nailed to the Cross*, rather than the usual Crucifixion (fig. 8). The vulnerable foreshortened figure of the Saviour is stretched out on the cross as executioners tug his feet straight and hammer in the nails. Beyond the main group, the gathering crowd overlooks the crest of Golgotha. This composition is distinctly reminiscent of the central panel from a small altarpiece in the National Gallery, painted by the Bruges artist Gerard David towards the end of the fifteenth century (fig. 86). Horenbout added a foreground row of figures, including the High Priest wearing a round hat and a red robe and mounted on an ass, like a Renaissance cardinal. The high viewpoint and this continuous circle of onlookers emphasise the isolation of the central victim.

Birago painted 18 decorated borders on pages of the Hours of the Cross. These follow a set pattern, with decorative panels flanking the lines of text, a small cartouche of text or picture at the top and a larger vignette at the foot of each page. At the tops of several pages, emblems refer to the earlier stages of the Passion: the Pelican in Piety (13r), 30 pieces of silver (15v), kiss of Judas (18r), washing of Pontius Pilate's hands (20r), Peter cutting off the ear of the servant of the High Priest (21r) and mocking of Christ (21v). These are followed by five half-length angels bearing the symbols of the Passion and St Veronica with the Sudarium. At the bottom of the decorated folios is a series of miniatures of chubby *putti*. These portray Isaac, whose intended sacrifice prefigured that

41 Birago: *St John the Baptist*, Suffrages (fol. 187v).

42 Birago: *St Peter*, Suffrages
(fol. 188v).

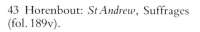

43 Horenbout: *St Andrew*, Suffrages
(fol. 189v).

44 Birago: *St James the Greater*, Suffrages (fol. 190v).

45 Birago: *St Stephen*, Suffrages (fol. 191v).

of Christ (13r), followed by Apostles and figures associated with the Crucifixion, including Peter (13v), Barnabas (14v, *see* fig. 9), Paul (15v), Joseph of Arimathea (16v), Nicodemus (17v), John the Evangelist (18r), Longinus (19r), Simon (20r), Thomas (22r), James the Greater (23r), Bartholomew (25r) and Philip (27r). These lively little scenes constitute a discursive supplement to the central theme of the Crucifixion.

THE HOURS OF THE HOLY SPIRIT

Birago's decoration of this section of the manuscript, which appears to have survived completely intact, opens with a full page miniature of *Pentecost* on fol. 28r (fig. 10). This depicts the miraculous event recorded in Acts 2.2–4:

And suddenly there came a sound from heaven as of a rushing mighty wind... And there appeared unto them cloven tongues like as of fire, and it sat upon each of them. And they were all filled with the Holy Ghost, and began to speak with other tongues, as the Spirit gave them utterance.

The Virgin Mary and the Apostles are depicted kneeling in prayer to witness this descent of the Holy Ghost, personified as a dove.

This miniature is followed by the most exquisite cycle of decorated borders in the Sforza Hours. Birago characterised the 'sound from heaven' as a chorus of celestial music performed by an orchestra of half-length musical angels in 17 vignettes, accompanied by a lesser number of *putti* and doves symbolic of the Holy Spirit. His brilliant musical analogy, so appropriate for a prayer book, is sustained by variation in the poses of the angels and the types of musical instruments which they play (fig. 11). Attired in gorgeous costumes of flame red, crimson, blue and green, the musicians have flowing wiry locks, reminiscent of the hair of figures in paintings by Birago's contemporary at the Sforza court, Leonardo da Vinci (fig. 87).

THE HOURS OF THE VIRGIN

The Little Office of the Virgin Mary, usually known as the Hours of the Virgin, is a series of eight sets of prayers, intended to be read at the different Hours of the day specified by Church liturgy. It constitutes the heart of all books of hours and was usually the part with the most elaborate decoration. Doubtless for this reason, this part of the Sforza Hours seems to have suffered particularly severely from Fra Joanne Jacopo's theft and nearly half of it comprises replacement folios made for Margaret of Austria. Conclusive proof that this section has been mutilated, rather than merely left unfinished, was provided in 1941 by the discovery of Birago's miniature of the *Adoration of the Magi* (British Library, Add. MS 45722, *see* fig. 20) which originally opened Sext, its fifth Hour, or section.

Horenbout painted miniatures opening each of the eight Hours. These comprise the customary Infancy Cycle of seven pictures tracing the story of the Virgin from the Annunciation through to the Flight into Egypt, plus a miniature of the *Coronation of the Virgin*. This cycle is notable for the dramatic miraculous lighting effects in the

Annunciation on fol. 41r (fig. 12), the *Nativity, at Night* on fol. 82v (fig. 17) and the *Annunciation to the Shepherds* on fol. 91r (fig. 19), which belong to a tradition initiated by the Netherlandish painters Hugo van der Goes and Geertgen tot Sint Jans during the late fifteenth century. The *Visitation* on fol. 61r (fig. 15) includes a portrait of Margaret of Austria, recognisable from her portraits by Conrad Meit and Bernart van Orley, in the guise of St Elizabeth greeting the Virgin. At their feet are scattered coloured pebbles – a motif derived from Birago's earlier miniatures. In the background, craggy hills allude to St Luke's location of the meeting in 'the hill country', but the sumptuous mansion and gatehouse in Renaissance style are more evocative of Margaret's palace at Malines than the 'city of Juda' where St Elizabeth lived.

Although all of Birago's full-page miniatures were removed from the Hours of the Virgin, it retains the longest series of decorated borders in the manuscript. These are of uneven quality. Some decorated text pages, such as fol. 54r where the vertical borders are composed of Bona's emblem of the peacock, are amongst the finest in the book (fig. 14). One, fol. 113r, appears to have been painted by a Ferrarese-trained artist, imitating the layout of Birago's borders but not his style. Others have a lighter palette than that usually employed by the master, suggesting the participation of workshop

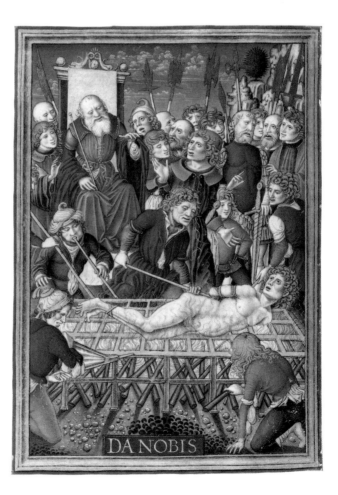

46 Birago: *St Lawrence*, Suffrages (fol. 192v).

(*Above, left*)
47 Birago: *St Sebastian*, Suffrages (fol. 193v).

(*Above, right*)
48 Birago: *St Julian*, Suffrages (fol. 194v).

(*Right*)
49 Birago: *St George*, Suffrages (fol. 195v).

(*Above, left*)
50 Birago: *St Gregory*, Suffrages (fol. 196v).

(*Above, right*)
51 Birago: *St Jerome*, Suffrages (fol. 197v).

(*Right*)
52 Birago: *St Ambrose*, Suffrages (fol. 198v).

assistants. On fols 51r, 53r, 73r (*see* fig. 16), 90r and 95v, script and decoration are reconciled illusionistically, with the text rendered as though inscribed upon a tabernacle. There are numerous marginal pictures of animals, some of which have emblematic associations with Bona and the Sforza, and bust portraits appear in several borders. It is unclear if the latter include likenesses of actual individuals but they may have profoundly impressed Horenbout, whose son Lucas became an early practitioner of the portrait miniature at the Tudor Court. Horenbout's interest in Birago's decorated text pages is evident from his imitation of one on fol. 48r (*see* fig. 13).

THE PASSION ACCORDING TO ST LUKE

Nearly half the folios in this text of St Luke 22.1–23.53 are replacements, but Horenbout's opening miniature of the *Entry into Jerusalem* on fol. 136v (*see* fig. 26) illustrates a slightly earlier part of the Gospel, so Birago's Passion cycle would appear to be complete. To provide a fuller account of the story, it employs continuous narrative. Thus, 'Then entered Satan into Judas' (St Luke 22.3) is depicted in the background of the *Payment of Judas* on fol. 137r (*see* fig. 27), which relates how the traitor 'communed with the chief priests and captains, how he might betray him unto them. And they were glad, and covenanted to give him money' (St Luke 22.4–5). Similarly, two tiny pictures of Christ's instructions to Peter and John to follow a man with a pitcher of water to the house where the Passover was to be celebrated appear in the background of the *Last Supper* on fol. 138v (*see* fig. 28). This is one of Birago's most sophisticated compositions, which transforms the customary lateral disposition of the subject into a series of tiers, clearly distinguishing the central drama from the subsidiary groups of servants and the supplementary scenes.

Additional events are also included in the backgrounds of the *Arrest of Christ* on fol. 147v (Christ saying 'I am he' to the 'men and officers from the chief priests and Pharisees' upon which 'they went backward, and fell to the ground' – St John 18.3–6), fig. 30, *Christ before Annanias* on fol. 149v (Christ's legendary Farewell to the Virgin and St Peter's Denial of Christ), fig. 31, *Christ before Caiaphas* on fol. 151v (the Flagellation), fig. 32, and the *Ecce Homo* on fol. 153v (Pilate watching the Crowning with Thorns and Christ before Herod), fig. 33. These four miniatures portray Christ's tormentors as dark-skinned, bestial and plagued by boils. The ugliness of this terrifying crowd exceeds that of the often monstrous executioners encountered in late fifteenth-century northern engravings, suggesting that Birago may also have had access to the grotesque caricatures of Leonardo da Vinci. The pent-up emotion of the Passion series reaches its peak with a *Crucifixion* overcrowded to the point of claustrophobia on fol. 161r (*see* fig. 34). In the final miniature, the *Pieta* (with the Resurrection and the Descent into Limbo in the background) on fol. 165r (*see* fig. 35), the Virgin's histrionic gesture of despair is echoed by the agitated drapery folds of the foreground figures.

SEVEN PRAYERS OF ST GREGORY, 'OBSECRO TE' AND 'O INTEMERATA'

The short Seven Prayers of St Gregory are a series of exclamations to Christ on the cross, traditionally ascribed to this Pope and Father of the Church, which he was believed to have uttered when a miracle occurred whilst he was celebrating mass. One of his acolytes doubted the real presence of Christ in the Host, causing an apparition of the Saviour on the altar. In Birago's prefatory miniature of this legend on fol.167r (*see* fig. 36), Christ is depicted in the traditional guise of the Man of Sorrows surrounded by implements of, and emblematic events from, the Passion. The vignettes in the decorated borders around the following text of the Prayers depict additional Passion scenes: the Man of Sorrows and the crucified Christ given vinegar (fol.167v), Three Maries at the tomb (fol.168r), 'Noli Me Tangere' and Christ on the Cross (fol.168v), Descent into Limbo (fol.169r) and the Ascension (fol.169v).

Although three-quarters of the folios in the prayers to the Virgin 'Obsecro te' and 'O intemerata' are replacements, Birago's introductory miniature to the former on fol.170r has survived (figs 37, 38). It depicts the Ascension of the Virgin, accompanied by musical angels and *putti*, above the astonished heads of the apostles and before a beautiful Po

53 Birago: *St Augustine*, Suffrages
(fol. 199v).

(*Above, left*)
54 Birago: *St Bernard*, Suffrages (fol. 200v).

(*Above, right*)
55 Birago: *St Henry the Bishop*, Suffrages (fol. 201v).

(*Left*)
56 Birago: *St Anthony*, Suffrages (fol. 202v).

(*Right*)
57 Birago: *St Anthony*, Suffrages (fol. 202v [enlarged]).

OMNIPOTENS

valley landscape with a fortified town. This subject, with the Virgin poised between Heaven and Earth, emphasises the prayer's appeal to her as an intercessor for Mankind. The figure in the left background is St Thomas who, according to legend, sceptically refused to believe the miracle before his eyes, until the Virgin cast him her girdle as proof. Horenbout's miniature of the *Virgin and Child* on fol.177v (*see* fig.39), opening the prayers 'O intemerata', recalls contemporary altarpieces by Italianate Antwerp painters such as Joos van Cleve which also portray the Virgin on a throne of Renaissance form, flanked by musical angels (fig.85).

THE SUFFRAGES OF THE SAINTS

Birago's 25 miniatures illustrating this series of short prayers to major saints is the finest cycle of decoration in the Sforza Hours. It seems to be substantially intact, Horenbout's sole addition being the miniature of the patron saint of Burgundy, *St Andrew*, on fol.189v (*see* fig.43). The saints are arranged, males before females, in order of importance. Accordingly, the Archangel Michael (fig.40) is followed by John the Baptist (fig.41), Apostles (figs 42–44), Martyrs (figs 45–49), Fathers of the Church (figs 50–53), monks

58 Birago: *St Giles the Abbot*, Suffrages (fol.203v).

44

and confessors (figs 54–58), friars (figs 59–62), St Catherine (fig. 63) and nuns (figs 64, 65). The last of the series, St Mary Magdalene on fol. 211v (*see* figs 66, 67), has been misplaced and should properly head the Suffrages for female saints.

Instead of merely portraying the saints with their attributes, Birago has enlivened the series by depicting miracles, martyrdoms and other key events in their stories. St John baptises Christ in the river Jordan (fig. 41) and St James baptises his executioners (fig. 44). St Julian (fig. 48) realises with horror that he has killed his own parents and a child compares St Augustine's attempts to explain the mystery of the Trinity with trying to empty the sea into a little hole (fig. 53). St Bernardino is confronted by the mitres of the three bishoprics he refused (fig. 62) and St Clare repels an attack upon her convent with a monstrance (fig. 65). St Mary Magdalene is portrayed in later life as a hermit, covered by her own flowing hair, being carried by angels to heaven for nourishment (fig. 66). In the background appears the pilgrim whose wife she restored to life and whose child she protected after they were abandoned. Some motifs, such as the rabbits in the miniatures of *St Gregory* (fig. 50) and *St Catherine of Siena* (fig. 64) and the peacock in that of *St Henry the Bishop* (fig. 55), are probably emblems of Bona and the Sforza rather than attributes of saints.

59 Birago: *St Albert of Trapani*, Suffrages (fol. 204v).

60 Birago: *St Peter Martyr*, Suffrages (fol. 205v).

61 Birago: *St Francis*, Suffrages (fol. 206v).

62 Birago: *St Bernardino of Siena*,
Suffrages (fol. 207v).

63 Birago: *St Catherine*, Suffrages
(fol. 208v).

Throughout the Suffrages, Mantegna's influence (fig. 84) is evident in Birago's predeliction for landscapes composed of rocky heaps of striated boulders interspersed with formalised trees and distant buildings, as well as in the antique cuirasses worn by his warrior saints and pagan soldiers. Two famous early engravings may have inspired the chimeras which assault St Anthony on fol. 202v: Mantegna's *Battle of Sea Gods* and Schongauer's *Temptation of St Anthony*. In the miniature of *St Catherine* on fol. 208v (*see* fig. 63), the foreshortened corpse at the bottom right is Mantegnesque, while the wiry mane and 'nutcracker' profile of the ragged executioner with a halter at the left recall Leonardo's caricatures.

Birago's spirited use of colour contrasts, especially between dark blue, crimson, flame red and dark green, imbues these miniatures with life and clarifies their narrative content. The bond between St George and the princess he has rescued on fol. 195v (*see* fig. 49) is expressed by the dark blue costume with flame-coloured sleeves which they both wear and by their long flowing gold hair. In the *Stoning of St Stephen* on fol. 191v, the crimson attire of his assailants forms a threatening crescent enveloping the martyr's flame-coloured dalmatic, which is echoed by the red robe of the blessing Christ at top left (fig. 45). On fol. 186v in *St Michael* (fig. 40), the gradual transformation of the background sky from ultramarine to yellowish green denotes the effect of aerial perspective and emphasises the descent of the fallen angels, as these colours reappear in the cuirass of the archangel and the hide of the recumbent devil beneath his feet.

THE SEVEN PENITENTIAL PSALMS AND THE LITANY

The Penitential Psalms (6, 32, 38, 51, 102, 130 and 143 in the King James Bible) were codified in the sixth century. King David was popularly believed to be the author of the psalms and was especially associated with repentence because of his contrition when rebuked by Nathan for causing the death of Uriah the Hittite in order to marry his beautiful wife Bathsheba (II Samuel. 11–12). For this reason, this text is often preceded by a miniature of David in Penitence. In the Sforza Hours, which is one of the most richly decorated prayer books of the Renaissance, each of the psalms has a prefatory full-page picture of this subject.

Over a third of this section comprises replacement folios, but six of Birago's miniatures survive. To mitigate the repetitiveness of their subject-matter, Birago varied each composition, depicting David as a king (fol. 218r, *see* fig. 72), being taken to task by Nathan (fol. 223r, *see* fig. 73) and as a penitent hermit in the wilderness (fol. 227r, *see* fig. 74). Moreover, the miniatures include lively details, such as the ermines at the bottom right and the fisherman reflected in the background pond of that on fol. 232r (*see* fig. 75). Horenbout's *King David in Penitence* on fol. 212v (figs 68, 69) portrays David in the porch of a palace, his attributes of a harp, sceptre and crown scattered in disarray, with hands clasped in terrified supplication as he sinks to his knees before an apparition of God and an avenging angel. The background scene of David enthroned at a loggia, administering the justice he had denied Uriah to a straggling crowd of supplicants admitted to the palace courtyard, lends point to his predicament.

Directly opposite this miniature, on fol. 213r (fig. 70), a page with rich borders opens the text of the Penitential Psalms. Most of its decoration is by Birago, but Horenbout added to the bottom border a gold oval portrait medallion of the youthful Emperor Charles V with the date 1520 inscribed on its upper rim. This is flanked by the fourfold monogram *K.I.* for 'Karolus Imperator' and a pair of beautifully painted gilt glass vases, whose feet cast an illusionistic circular shadow across the bottom edge of the border.

The Litany, which normally follows the Penitential Psalms, is a call for mercy invoking the Trinity, the Virgin Mary and many saints. Although not usually illustrated, on fol. 236r of the Sforza Hours (fig. 77) it is prefaced with a full-page miniature of the institution of the Great Litany by Pope Gregory the Great in 590. It was believed that as the Romans had previously observed Lent and then indulged themselves, they were punished by the plague. In expiation, Pope Gregory arranged penances and a great procession through Rome and introduced the Litany. Birago's miniature depicts the Pope, clergy and people kneeling before St Michael sheathing a sword, as a sign that God's anger had been appeased. This apparition was believed to have occurred on the mausoleum of Hadrian, subsequently converted into a fortress and known thereafter as the Castel Sant'Angelo, which appears in the left background. More than half the folios

64 Birago: *St Catherine of Siena*, Suffrages (fol. 209v).

(*Above, left*)
65 Birago: *St Clare*, Suffrages
(fol. 210v).

(*Above, right*)
66 Birago: *St Mary Magdalene*, Suffrages
(fol. 211v).

(*Right*)
67 Birago: *St Mary Magdalene*, Suffrages
(fol. 211v [detail]).

(*Above, left*)
68 Horenbout: *King David in Penitence*, Penitential Psalms (fol. 212v).

(*Right*)
69 Horenbout: *King David in Penitence*, Penitential Psalms (fol. 212v [detail]).

(*Above, right*)
70 Birago and Horenbout: Decorated border with vignette of Charles V, Penitential Psalms (fol. 213r).

71 Birago: *King David in Penitence*,
Penitential Psalms (fol. 215r).

72 Birago: *King David in Penitence*,
Penitential Psalms (fol. 218r).

73 Birago: *King David in Penitence*,
Penitential Psalms (fol. 223r).

74 Birago: *King David in Penitence*,
Penitential Psalms (fol. 227r).

53

75 Birago: *King David in Penitence,*
Penitential Psalms (fol. 232r).

76 Birago: *King David in Penitence,*
Penitential Psalms (fol. 233v).

KIRIELEYSON

77 Birago: *Procession of St Gregory*,
Litany (fol. 236r).

THEODORINA LONGO
BARDORꝪ REGINA · V · P ·

78 Birago: Decorated border with
vignette of Queen Theodelinda of the
Lombards, Litany (fol. 255r).

in the Litany are replacements, so Birago's half-length vignettes at the foot of its surviving decorated borders are probably a fraction of the original series. These depict Old Testament heroines and female saints: Deborah, the prophetess who incited Barak to attack Sisera (fol. 251r), Esther the wife of King Ahasuerus (fol. 251v), Judith who decapitated Holofernes (fol. 252r), Anne 'widow and prophetess', presumably the mother of the Virgin (fol. 252v), Theodelinda, first christian queen of the Lombards (fol. 255r, *see* fig. 78), St Pelagia the Penitent (fol. 255v) and St Elizabeth of Hungary (fol. 256r).

THE OFFICE OF THE DEAD

It was customary to include in books of hours the prayers said over a coffin during the vigil before burial, as these were frequently read as a form of private devotion, emphasising the inevitability of death. Traditionally the office had a single large miniature of a deathbed scene, but a wider range of subject matter developed during the fifteenth century. This included the *Raising of Lazarus* (St John 11.1–46), depicted by Horenbout facing the start of the office on fol. 257v of the Sforza Hours (fig. 79). In response to Christ's admonition 'Lazarus, come forth', the dead man emerges from his

79 Horenbout: *Raising of Lazarus*, Office of the Dead (fol. 257v).

grave as St Peter unties his hands, which have been bound in an attitude of prayer. At the bottom right kneel Lazarus's sisters, the richly dressed St Mary Magdalene and the plainer housewife St Martha. The astounded Jews at the left include one raising his sleeve to his mouth, alluding to Martha's warning 'he stinketh: for he hath been dead four days'. Behind the biblical scene is a great Flemish church with romanesque transepts and a gothic choir.

Nearly a third of the folios in the Office of the Dead are replacements, suggesting that its numerous decorated borders, exceeded only by those in the Hours of the Virgin, are no more than a fragment of the series planned by Birago. Some vignettes are inhabited by animals, including the emblematic ermine and phoenix, playful *putti*, a diminutive nereid, triton and centaur, musical angels and biblical figures. One, on fol. 306v, depicting a finely dressed young gentleman giving alms to a beggar, directly illustrates the text praising charity on the same page. The principal theme of these borders is introduced on the opening text page, fol. 258r (fig. 80), by a reclining *putto* contemplating a death's head infested by a snake. This startling image and the numerous other vignettes of bones, skulls with snakes crawling out of eye sockets and *putti* wrestling with serpents are unambiguous references to mortality.

The single full-page miniature by Birago in the Office, the *Death of the Virgin* on fol. 272r (fig. 81), may be a survivor of a more elaborate programme. This subject, often included in the Hours of the Virgin as an illustration to Compline, the last of the eight Hours, rarely appears in the Office of the Dead. An apocryphal subject dating from the fourth century, it is appropriate in this context as an example to the Christian of how to make a good end. Having been told by an angel that she had not long to live, the Virgin calmly lay down facing east to await death. She was attended by the Apostles, who are depicted as old men, some wearing spectacles. In the centre St Peter administers the last rites. Wearing a priest's cope, he reads from the prayer book and sprinkles holy water, whilst his colleagues swing a censer, intone the service, bless the Virgin and wipe tears from their eyes.

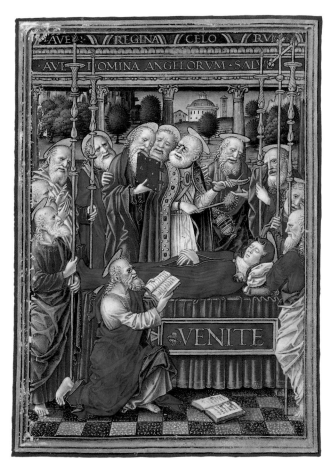

(*Above, left*)
80 Birago: Decorated border with vignette of a *putto* holding a skull, Office of the Dead (fol. 258r).

(*Above, right*)
81 Birago: *Death of the Virgin*, Office of the Dead (fol. 272r).

(*Left*)
82 Birago: Decorated border with musical angels, Office of the Dead (fol. 334r).

(*Right*)
83 Birago: Decorated border, Office of the Dead (fol. 341r [enlarged]).

Eus nenie 1
largito: 7 hu
mane salutis
amator quesum° clem
tiam tuam: ut nostre 1
congregationis fratre°
sorores parentes pro
pinquos et benefacto
res nostros qui ex hoc
seculo transierunt be
ata maria semper uir

84 Andrea Mantegna, *Agony in the Garden*, National Gallery, London. This panel painting of *c.*1460 is a fine example of Mantegna's lapidary and antiquarian style, so influential throughout later fifteenth century North Italy.

85 Joos van Cleve, *Virgin and Child with Angels*, Walker Art Gallery, Liverpool. This Italianate altarpiece of *c.*1520 reveals the distinct influence of Leonardo on Netherlandish painting.

86 Gerard David, *Christ nailed to the Cross*, National Gallery, London. The central panel of a small altarpiece, probably of the 1480s, typical of the Netherlandish school during Horenbout's youth.

87 Leonardo da Vinci, *Virgin of the Rocks*, National Gallery, London. Copied in *c*.1508 from Leonardo's altarpiece in the Louvre, commissioned in 1483, shortly after his arrival as court painter in Milan.

THE STRUCTURE AND CONTENTS OF THE SFORZA HOURS

BRITISH LIBRARY ADD. MS 34294

Use of Rome; vellum, 348 leaves; 13.1 × 9.3 cm.

Dark red morocco binding, c. 1896.

The leaves have been separated and tipped into 4 volumes. 64 full-page miniatures, 140 text pages with decorated borders and small miniatures, numerous decorated capitals, rounded gothic script.

Various inscriptions of Bona Sforza's name occur on several folios: *Diva Bona* on fols 66v, 79v and 122v; *Bona Duc*[issa] in the miniature on fol. 210v and *B.M.* on fol. 56r and 88v. On fol. 93r the motto *Sola fata, solum Deum sequor* combined with a phoenix.

In the miniature on fol. 10v the date 1519 with what may be a coded signature. In the *Visitation* on fol. 61r a portrait of Margaret of Austria as St Elizabeth. In the decorated border on fol. 213r a medallion with a portrait of Charles V and the date 1520.

Three additional detached miniatures are known, of which two are also in the British Library: Add. MS 45722, Add. MS 62997, and Coll. B. Breslauer, New York.

CALENDAR (fragmentary)

Full-page miniatures by Birago of *May* (British Library Add. MS 62997r) and *October* (Coll. B. Breslauer, New York).

GOSPEL LESSONS

Fols 1r–12r (of which fols 3, 6 and 9–12 are replacements).

Full-page miniatures by Birago of *St John* on fol. 1r, *St Luke* on fol. 4r and *St Matthew* on fol. 7r and by Horenbout of *St Mark* on fol. 10v.

HOURS OF THE CROSS

Fols 12v–27v (of which fol. 12 is a replacement).

Full-page miniature by Horenbout of *Christ nailed to the Cross* on fol. 12v.

Eighteen decorated borders by Birago; fols 13r–13v, 14v, 15v, 16v, 17v, 18r, 19r–19v, 20r, 21r–21v, 22r, 23r, 24r, 25r, 26r and 27r.

HOURS OF THE HOLY SPIRIT

Fols 28r–40v.

Full-page miniature by Birago of the *Descent of the Holy Spirit* on fol. 28r.

Twenty-one decorated borders by Birago; fols 29r–37r, 38r–38v, 39v–40r.

HOURS OF THE VIRGIN

Fols 41r–133r (of which fols 41, 48, 60–61, 65, 68–69, 72, 82–83, 86–87, 91, 94, 97–99, 102–04, 106, 111, 114–19, 121, 124–25 and 128–33 are replacements).

Full-page miniatures by Horenbout of the *Annunciation* on fol. 41r, *Visitation* on fol. 61r, *Nativity, at Night* on fol. 82v, *Annunciation to the Shepherds* on fol. 91r, *Adoration of the Magi* on fol. 97r, *Presentation in the Temple* on fol. 104v, *Flight into Egypt* on fol. 111r and *Coronation of the Virgin by the Trinity* on fol. 124r. The original full-page miniature by Birago of the *Adoration of the Magi* also exists (British Library, Add. MS. 45722r).

Forty-four decorated borders by Birago; fols 42r, 45r, 46r, 51r, 53r, 54r, 55r, 56r, 58r, 62r, 63r, 64v, 66v, 67v, 71r, 73r, 74v, 75v–76r, 77r, 79v, 80v–81r, 84v, 85v, 88r–89r, 90r–90v, 93r, 95v, 96v, 101r, 105r, 107v, 108v, 109v–110v, 122v, 123v, 126r and 127r, 1 decorated border by a Ferrarese-trained painter; fol. 113r and 1 decorated border by Horenbout; fol. 48r.

THE ACCESSORY PRAYER 'SALVE REGINA'

Fols 133v–136r (all of which are replacements).

Full-page miniature by Horenbout of the *Virgin and Child in Glory* on fol. 133v.

PASSION ACCORDING TO ST LUKE

Fols 136v–166v (of which fols 136, 139–42, 154–59, 163 and 166 are replacements).

Full-page miniatures by Horenbout of the *Entry into Jerusalem* on fol. 136v and by Birago of the *Payment of Judas* on fol. 137r, *Last Supper* on fol. 138v, *Agony in the Garden* on fol. 145v, *Arrest of Christ* on fol. 147v, *Christ before Annanias* on fol. 149v, *Christ before Caiaphas* on fol. 151v, *Ecce Homo* on fol. 153v, *Crucifixion* on fol. 161r and *Pieta* on fol. 165r.

SEVEN PRAYERS OF ST GREGORY

Fols 167r–169v.

Full-page miniature by Birago of the *Mass of St Gregory* on fol. 167r.

Five decorated borders by Birago; fols 167r–169v.

'OBSECRO TE', 'O INTEMERATA'

Fols 170r–186r (of which fols 171–74 and 177–85 are replacements).

Full-page miniatures by Birago of the *Assumption of the Virgin* on fol. 170r and by Horenbout of the *Virgin and Child* on fol. 177v.

SUFFRAGES OF THE SAINTS

Fols 186r–212r (of which fol. 189 is a replacement).

Full-page miniatures by Birago of *St Michael* on fol. 186v, *St John the Baptist* on fol. 187v and *St Peter* on fol. 188v, by Horenbout of *St Andrew* on fol. 189v and by Birago of *St James the Greater* on fol. 190v, *St Stephen* on fol. 191v, *St Lawrence* on fol. 192v, *St Sebastian* on fol. 193v, *St Julian* on fol. 194v, *St George* on fol. 195v, *St Gregory the Great* on fol. 196v, *St Jerome* on fol. 197v, *St Ambrose* on fol. 198v, *St Augustine* on fol. 199v, *St Bernard* on fol. 200v, *St Henry the Bishop* on fol. 201v, *St Anthony* on fol. 202v, *St Giles the Abbot* on fol. 203v, *St Albert of Trapani* on fol. 204v, *St Peter Martyr* on fol. 205v, *St Francis* on fol. 206v, *St Bernardino of Siena* on fol. 207v, *St Catherine* on fol. 208v, *St Catherine of Siena* on fol. 209v, *St Clare* on fol. 210v and *St Mary Magdalene* on fol. 211v.

SEVEN PENITENTIAL PSALMS

Fols 212v–235v (of which fols 217, 221, 225–26, 228–29 and 234–35 are replacements).

Full-page miniature by Horenbout of *King David in Penitence* on fol. 212v and by Birago of the same subject on fols 215r, 218r, 223r, 227r, 232r and 233v.

One decorated border by Birago and Horenbout; fol. 213r.

LITANY

Fols 236r–257r (of which fols 237–42, 244, 247, 250, 253–54 and 257 are replacements).

Full-page miniature by Birago of the *Procession of St Gregory* on fol. 236r.

Eight decorated borders by Birago; fols 248r, 251r–252v and 255r–256r.

OFFICE OF THE DEAD

Fols 257v–342v (of which fols 257, 274, 276, 278–79, 281–82, 289, 291, 295–96, 298, 300, 303, 305, 307–08, 311–12, 315, 317–18, 320, 330 and 337–38 are replacements).

Full-page miniatures by Horenbout of the *Raising of Lazarus* on fol. 257v and by Birago of the *Death of the Virgin* on fol. 272r.

Forty-one decorated borders by Birago; fols 258r, 259v, 261r, 262v, 263v, 266r, 267v, 269v, 270r, 271r–271v, 275r, 280r, 283v, 285r, 287r, 288v, 290r, 294r, 297v, 299r, 301r, 302r, 306v, 309v, 313r, 314v, 316v, 319v, 323r, 326r, 327v, 329r, 332r, 334r, 335r, 336v, 339r, 340v, 341r and 341v.

PRAYER OF THE NAME OF JESUS FROM THE EPISTLES OF ST PAUL

Fols 343r–348v. An unillustrated addition of around 1600.

FURTHER READING

Although nearly a century old, the only previous monograph on the Sforza Hours remains essential reading, G. F. Warner, *Miniatures and Borders from the Book of Hours of Bona Sforza, Duchess of Milan in the British Museum*, London 1894. The monumental, standard work on art in Milan during the late fifteenth century is F. Malaguzzi Valeri, *La Corte di Ludovico il Moro*, 4 vols, Milan 1913–23. For the history of the Sforza Hours see the picaresque account of its discovery by J. C. Robinson, 'The Sforza Book of Hours', *Bibliographica* I, 1895, pp. 428–36 and the documents relating to its creation printed in G. Mongeri, 'L'Arte del minio nel ducato di Milano dal secolo XII al XVI', *Archivio Storico Lombardo* 12, 1885, pp. 541–42, J. Duverger, 'Gerard Horenbault (1465?–1540): Hofschilder van Margareta van Oostenrijk', *De Kunst. Maandblad voor Oude en Jonge Kunst* I, 1930, pp. 81–90 and R. Flower, 'Margaret of Austria and the Sforza Book', *British Museum Quarterly* 10, 1935–36, pp. 100–02. For the identification of Giovan Pietro Birago as the Master of the Sforza Hours see B. Horodyski, 'Birago, Miniaturiste des Sforza', *Scriptorium* 10, 1956, pp. 251–55 and *Arte lombarda dai Visconti agli Sfroza*, Palazzo Reale, Milan 1958, pp. 141–45. More recent research on Birago, Horenbout and the Sforza Hours will be found in P. Wescher, 'F. Binasco, Miniaturmaler des Sforza', *Jahrbuch der Berliner Museen*, NS II, 1960, pp. 80–82, *Catalogue of Additions to the Manuscripts 1936–1945*, British Museum, London 1970, 2 vols, pp. 231–32, T. Kren (ed.), *Renaissance Painting in Manuscripts*, New York and London 1983, pp. 107–22, R. W. Scheller, 'Gallia cisalpina: Louis XII and Italy 1499–1508', *Simiolus* 15, 1, 1985, pp. 16–17, M. L. Evans, 'A Newly discovered leaf of "The Sforza Hours"', *British Library Journal* 12, 1, Spring 1986, pp. 21–27, L. Campbell and S. Foister, 'Gerard, Lucas and Susanna Horenbout', *Burlington Magazine* 128, 1003, October 1986, pp. 719–27, M. L. Evans, 'New Light on the "Sforziada" Frontispieces of Giovan Pietro Birago', *British Library Journal* 13, 2, Autumn 1987, pp. 232–47 and J. Backhouse, 'Illuminated Manuscripts and the Early Development of the Portrait Miniature', *Early Tudor England* (ed. D. Williams), Woodbridge 1989, pp. 1–17. Some account of Belbello da Pavia and earlier Milanese manuscript illumination is provided by C. Mitchell, *A Fifteenth Century Italian Plutarch*, London 1961 and M. Meiss and E. W. Kirsch, *The Visconti Hours*, London 1972. For the late fifteenth-century Florentine books of hours of Lorenzo de' Medici see M. L. Evans, *Die Miniaturen des Münchener Medici-Gebetbuchs Clm 23639 und verwandte Handschriften* in *Das Gebetbuch Lorenzos de' Medici*, Stuttgart 1991, pp. 167–272. Much useful supplementary information on Renaissance art may be found in D. S. Chambers, *Patrons and Artists in the Italian Renaissance*, London and Basingstoke 1970, M. Baxandall, *Painting and Experience in Fifteenth Century Italy*, Oxford 1972 and J. Dunkerton, S. Foister, D. Gordon and N. Penny, *Giotto to Dürer. Early Renaissance Painting in The National Gallery*, New Haven and London 1991. Two general accounts of Italian Renaissance illumination are J. J. G. Alexander, *Italian Renaissance Illuminations*, London 1977 and F. Avril (ed.), *Dix Siècles d'enluminure italienne*, Paris 1984, pp. 109–83. Up-to-date studies of books of hours include J. Harthan, *Books of Hours and their Owners*, London 1977, J. Backhouse, *Books of Hours*, London 1985 and R. S. Wieck, *The Book of hours in Medieval Art and Life*, London 1988.